DAUGHTERS
of the Revolution

by Myka-Lynne Sokoloff
illustrated by Bruce Emmett

Harcourt
SCHOOL PUBLISHERS

p.4, ©Library of Congress; p.6, ©Library of Congress; p.8, ©Dorlene Bordwell; p.12, ©US Army Women's Museum.

Copyright © by Harcourt, Inc.

Printed in China

ISBN 13: 978-0-15-350545-4
ISBN 10: 0-15-350545-1

Ordering Options
ISBN 13: 978-0-15-350335-1 (Grade 5 Below-Level Collection)
ISBN 10: 0-15-350335-1 (Grade 5 Below-Level Collection)
ISBN 13: 978-0-15-357543-3 (package of 5)
ISBN 10: 0-15-357543-3 (package of 5)

11 12 13 14 15   0940   12 11 10

The Revolutionary War was fought and won by a great many people working together. You may know the roles played by men such as George Washington, Thomas Jefferson, Ben Franklin, and John Adams. However, not as many people are familiar with the ways women helped to secure our country's freedom.

The lives of women in the 1700s were very different from those of women today. Women could not vote. Few had much schooling. It's no wonder, then, that we know little about the women who aided the war efforts. We don't know what many of these heroes looked like. In many cases, we don't even know their names.

Familiar faces of the Revolutionary War

Most of the women we do know about had special connections. Some were wives or daughters of important men. Still, those of note and those who were nameless all helped in the crisis that would shape this country's destiny.

Daughters of Liberty

Beginning in 1767, the British king made the colonists pay taxes on several items. The colonists felt the taxes were unfair. What bothered the colonists most? They had no say in how they were governed by the British.

A group of men called the Sons of Liberty held meetings and spoke out against the British. This group included John Hancock, John Adams, Paul Revere, and other patriots.

Another group called the Daughters of Liberty is less well-known. Many women, mostly under the age of forty, belonged to this group. These women led the boycott against British goods. They met together to spin yarn and weave cloth. This way, they would not need to buy British cloth.

Even Martha Washington took part in the boycott. Her home in Mount Vernon, Virginia, had sixteen spinning wheels running at one time. Both General Washington and Martha wore homespun cloth. To make her dresses look a bit more special, Lady Washington added pieces of silk torn from old chair seats.

Martha Washington

The Daughters of Liberty refused to buy English tea. They served "liberty tea" instead, made from herbs such as catnip or raspberry leaves.

The perseverance of the colonists paid off. In 1770, the British lifted many of the taxes. They did this even before the first shot of the war was fired. However, the tax on tea remained.

Sarah Bradlee Fulton was a Daughter of Liberty. She was known as the Mother of the Boston Tea Party. She invited some patriots into her home on December 16, 1773. There she painted men's faces with burnt cork. The men disguised themselves. That way they would not be recognized as they dumped chests of tea into Boston Harbor. After the Boston Tea Party, the men returned to Sarah's home to remove their disguises.

The Daughters of Liberty were not the only women who made a crucial difference in the fight for independence.

Phoebe Fraunces (1763 – Unknown)

Phoebe Fraunces was the daughter of an African American tavern owner in New York City. Fraunces Tavern was a favorite meeting spot of the Sons of Liberty, including George Washington. In 1776, at the age of thirteen, a man told a secret to Phoebe, who worked at the tavern. The British had hired him to poison Washington. Before Washington could eat a dish of poisoned peas, Phoebe tossed it out the window.

Not much else is known about Phoebe Fraunces. However, she will always be remembered for saving the life of General Washington. Phoebe's act was a small one, but without her help, this country's history could have been very different.

Sybil Ludington
(1761–1839)

Danbury, Connecticut, was burning! On April 26, 1777, two thousand British soldiers burned nearly every place that stored grain or meat. They saved only those places that were owned by people who sided with the king.

Messengers on horseback were sent to gather colonial soldiers. Without their help, Danbury would have been destroyed. One messenger rode to the home of Colonel Henry Ludington. As a veteran of the French and Indian War, Ludington now led the local army. His soldiers were not ready to fight that night, though. They were at home, planting their spring crops.

The messenger and his horse were too tired to ride on to alert the farmers. Colonel Ludington had to stay home to meet the men who would assemble there. Sybil, the colonel's sixteen-year-old daughter, appealed to her father to let her go.

Through the night, Sybil's horse galloped down roads muddied by pouring rain. Sybil banged on the shutters of house after house to wake the sleeping farmers. By morning, four hundred men met at her father's home, ready to save Danbury. According to legend, Sybil was thanked for her heroism by George Washington himself.

Lydia Barrington Darragh (1729–1789)

In 1777, the British had control of the city of Philadelphia, Pennsylvania. On December 2, British general William Howe took command of Lydia Darragh's dining room for a meeting. There the British planned a secret attack on George Washington and the Continental Army at Whitemarsh, not far from Philadelphia. Although Lydia pretended to be asleep, she actually listened at the keyhole as the British made their plans.

Two days later, Lydia maneuvered her way out of town by persuading the British that she needed some flour to make bread. She was given a pass to walk to the mill.

On the way, Lydia encountered a friend, Colonel Thomas Craig. She shared the news of the secret attack. Then she purchased some flour and returned home. Forewarned, the colonial army was ready to fight when the British arrived at Whitemarsh. General Howe was pushed back to Philadelphia without firing a shot.

Deborah Samson
(1760–1827)

The fact that Deborah Samson was a woman did not stop her from fighting in the colonial army. Deborah had been born into a large family that had little money. When her father died, Deborah became a servant. She read the books of the children she cared for, and later she became a teacher.

When the Revolutionary War began, Deborah Samson was not content to spin yarn or nurse injured soldiers. In 1782, she dressed in men's clothing and took the name Robert Shurtleff. Then she enlisted in the army.

Samson was wounded a number of times. Afraid that doctors would learn she was a woman, Deborah tried to care for the wounds herself. A fever finally sent her to the doctor who discovered her secret.

Some stories suggest that "Robert Shurtleff" was once asked to deliver a message to General George Washington, a job that showed how much she was respected and trusted. Samson died in 1827. After she died, her family received a pension for Deborah's army service.

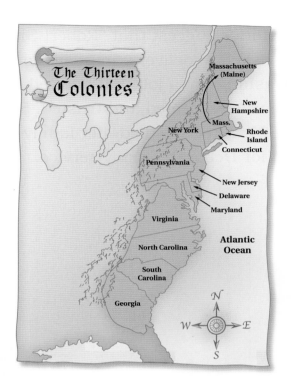

The Thirteen Colonies

Massachusetts (Maine)

New Hampshire

Mass.

New York

Rhode Island

Connecticut

Pennsylvania

New Jersey

Delaware

Maryland

Virginia

Atlantic Ocean

North Carolina

South Carolina

Georgia

N
W — E
S

Many women helped in small, quiet ways
to aid the American Revolution. Others took
greater risks. Some, like Lydia Darragh, spied
for the patriots. Sybil Ludington, one of the
youngest heroes of the Revolution, was not the
only woman to spread the alarm on horseback.
Several women like Deborah Samson joined in
battle. Little by little, the efforts of untold
women added together, helping the thirteen
colonies win the battle for independence.

Think Critically

1. Which events in this book took place before the Declaration of Independence was signed in 1776? Which events took place after?

2. How can you tell that this book is a nonfiction book?

3. How were the actions of women like Darragh and Samson different from those of the Daughters of Liberty?

4. How did the author organize the information in this book?

5. To which woman described in the book would you choose to give a medal? Why?

Social Studies

Create a Time Line Make a time line of the events described in this book. Include names of groups or individuals, dates, and a few words about each important event.

School-Home Connection Share this book with your family. Then talk with family members about women you know who have done heroic things.

Word Count: 1,211